W9-CHZ-024

Classifying Living Things

Invertebrates

Francine D. Galko

Chicago, Illinois

www.heinemannraintree.com
Visit our website to find out
more information about
Heinemann-Raintree books.

To order:
☎ Phone 888-454-2279
⌨ Visit www.heinemannraintree.com
to browse our catalog and order online.

© 2004, 2009 Heinemann Library
A division of Capstone Global Library LLC
Chicago, Illinois

Customer Service 888-454-2279

Visit our website at heinemannraintree.com

All rights reserved. No part of this publication may be
reproduced or transmitted in any form or by any means,
electronic or mechanical, including photocopying, recording,
taping, or any information storage and retrieval system,
without permission in writing from the publisher.

Edited by Catherine Clarke and Claire Throp
Designed by Victoria Bevan and AMR Design Ltd
Original illustrations © Capstone Global Library, LLC
Illustrations by Carrie Gowran
Picture research by Hannah Taylor
Originated by Steve Walker
Printed and bound in China by Leo Paper Group

13 12 11 10 09
10 9 8 7 6 5 4 3 2 1

Library of Congress Cataloging-in-Publication Data

Galko, Francine.
  Invertebrates / by Francine Galko.
    v. cm. -- (Classifying living things)
Includes bibliographical references and index.
Contents: The variety of life -- What are invertebrates?
-- Sponges -- Cnidarians -- Flatworms -- Roundworms --
Segmented worms -- Mollusks -- Arthropods -- Echinoderms
-- Organizing invertebrates
  ISBN 978 1 432923 59 4 (Hardcover) --
  ISBN 978 1 432923 69 3 (Paperback)
  1. Invertebrates--Juvenile literature.
[1. Invertebrates.] I. Title. II. Series.
  QL362.4.G34 2003
  592--dc21
                          2003004979

Acknowledgments

We would like to thank the following for permission to
reproduce photographs:

ardea.com pp. 7 (Steve Downer), 12 (Pat Morris); Corbis pp.
4 (Darrell Gulin), 5 (Robert Pickett), 6 (Jeffrey L. Rotman), 8
(James L. Amos), 13 (Stephen Frink), 24 (Ralph A. Clevenger),
25 (Papilio/Dennis Johnson), 26 (Micheal & Patricia Fogden);
FLPA p. 28l (Reinhard Dirscherl); Getty Images pp. 9 (Taxi/
Gary Bell), 21 (National Geographic/Darlyne A. Murawski),
29 (Photonica/Ross Rappaport); naturepl p. 19 (Tony Phelps);
Photolibrary pp. 14 (Marevision), 15 (Karen Gowlett-Holmes),
16 (OSF), 17 (Dennis Kunkel), 22 (Charles Bowman), 23
(Marevision), 28r (Howard Hall); Science Photo Library p. 18
(David Scharf).

Cover photograph of a harlequin shrimp (Hymenocera elegans)
with starfish, Indonesia, reproduced with permission of FLPA/
Colin Marshall.

We would like to thank Ann Fullick and Philip P. Parrillo of
The Field Museum for their invaluable assistance in the
preparation of this book.

Every effort has been made to contact copyright holders
of any material reproduced in this book. Any omissions
will be rectified in subsequent printings if notice is given
to the publisher.

Contents

Some words are shown in bold, **like this**. You can find out what they mean by looking in the glossary.

The natural world is full of an incredible variety of **organisms**. They range from tiny **bacteria**, too small to see, to giant redwood trees over 100 meters (328 feet) tall. With such a bewildering variety of life, it's hard to make sense of the living world. For this reason, scientists **classify** living things by sorting them into groups.

Classifying the living world

Sorting organisms into groups makes them easier to understand. Scientists try to classify living things in a way that tells you how closely one group is related to another. They look at everything about an organism, from its color and shape to the **genes** inside its **cells**. They even look at **fossils** to give them clues about how living things have changed over time. Then the scientists use all this information to sort the millions of different things into groups.

Scientists don't always agree about the group an organism belongs to, so they collect as much evidence as possible to find its closest relatives.

Coral reefs are home to many invertebrates. Notice how the anemones and starfish look very different from one another.

From kingdoms to species

Classification allows us to measure the **biodiversity** of the world. To begin the classification process, scientists divide living things into huge groups called **kingdoms**. For example, plants are in one kingdom, while animals are in another. There is some argument among scientists about how many kingdoms there are—at the moment most agree that there are five! Each kingdom is then divided into smaller groups called **phyla** (singular phylum), and the phyla are further divided into **classes**. The next subdivision is into **orders**. Within an order, organisms are grouped into **families** and then into a **genus** (plural genera), which contains a number of closely related **species**. A species is a single kind of organism, such as a mouse or a buttercup. Members of a species can **reproduce** and produce fertile offspring together.

Scientific names

Many living things have a common name, but these can cause confusion when the same organism has different names around the world. To avoid problems, scientists give every species a two-part Latin name, which is the same all over the world. The first part of the scientific name tells you the genus the organism belongs to. The second part tells you the exact species. The common earthworm, for example, is *Lumbricus terrestris*, while the dog tapeworm is *Dipylidium caninum*.

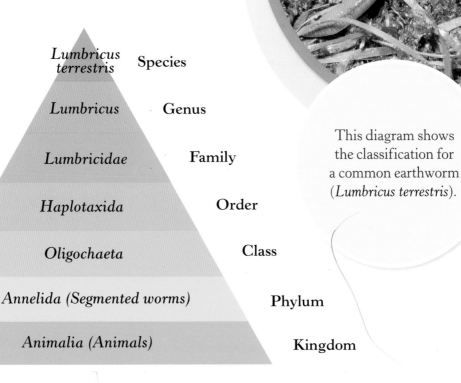

This diagram shows the classification for a common earthworm (*Lumbricus terrestris*).

Lumbricus terrestris	Species
Lumbricus	Genus
Lumbricidae	Family
Haplotaxida	Order
Oligochaeta	Class
Annelida (Segmented worms)	Phylum
Animalia (Animals)	Kingdom

What do worms, crabs, butterflies, and spiders all have in common? None of them has a backbone. This makes them invertebrates. In fact, most animals are invertebrates. The few animals that do have a backbone are called **vertebrates**. Humans, dogs, fish, frogs, snakes, and birds are vertebrates. All animals are **classified** as either invertebrates or vertebrates.

Many different kinds of animals are invertebrates. They range in size from a microscopic water flea to the giant squid. Invertebrates also live all over the world. Some, such as jellyfish and squid, live only in water, and others, such as bees, live on land only. Invertebrates include animals with very different bodies, too. Compare a hairy eight-legged spider, such as a tarantula, to a clam. Some invertebrates, such as millipedes, have many legs, and others, such as sponges, have no legs and cannot move from place to place.

Most sponges do not have a pattern. Sponges and other invertebrates that do not show a specific arrangement of body parts are asymmetric.

Body patterns

Symmetry means having a pattern. For example, your body has a right side and a left side. Your right side is a mirror image of your left side. There is only one way to divide your body into two mirror images: by drawing a line from the top of your head straight down to your feet. Animals that have two similar halves like you do are said to have **bilateral symmetry**. A butterfly is a good example of an invertebrate that is bilaterally symmetrical. Most invertebrates are bilaterally symmetrical.

Some invertebrates have **radial symmetry**. These animals grow in all directions from a central point. There is more than one way to divide their body into two mirror images. A starfish has radial symmetry. Other animals with radial symmetry include sand dollars and sea anemones.

Not all invertebrates have symmetry. Sponges are **asymmetric**. The parts of a sponge cannot be divided into two similar halves because they do not have a central point.

Jellyfish like this one have radial symmetry. Imagine a point in the center of this jellyfish's body. Any line that goes through this point will divide the animal's body into two similar halves.

Invertebrate skeletons

Many invertebrates, such as crabs, lobsters, and insects, have a hard skeleton on the outside of their body, protecting the soft **tissues** inside. This type of skeleton is called an **exoskeleton**. Exoskeletons have special joints and muscles so that the animal can move around. Exoskeletons make growing difficult, however. As the exoskeleton becomes a tight fit, the animal grows a new soft exoskeleton underneath. It sheds the too-small exoskeleton—this is called **molting**. The animal swells up to stretch the new exoskeleton until it has hardened. Then it can take time to grow and fill it up!

Some invertebrates have a **hydrostatic skeleton**. This kind of skeleton is formed by a sac inside the animal's body, which is filled with liquid. A hydrostatic skeleton works like a water balloon. The water inside the balloon makes the balloon firm. But when you squeeze a water balloon, the water moves and the shape of the balloon changes. Hydras and earthworms depend on hydrostatic skeletons to move about.

A few invertebrates have **endoskeletons**. An endoskeleton is a hard skeleton inside an animal's body. Your skeleton is a good example of an endoskeleton. Starfish also have an endoskeleton. Unlike your skeleton, though, starfish skeletons are not made of bones.

Many invertebrates, like this cicada, shed their exoskeleton as they outgrow it.

Tissues and organs

All invertebrates are **multicellular**. This means that they are made of many **cells** that work together to carry out basic life activities. To do this, the cells are specialized to carry out different jobs. A group of cells working together to carry out a certain job is called a tissue. A group of tissues working together make up an **organ**. Your heart is an organ made of muscle tissue, which pumps blood through your body. Many invertebrates have organs to carry out particular jobs.

Most invertebrates **digest** (break down) their food inside their bodies. Many invertebrates have a one-way gut with two openings: a mouth and an **anus**. Food enters the body through the mouth. Undigested food and other waste products leave the body through the anus. Roundworms have this kind of gut. Each step in digestion takes place with the help of specialized cells.

Most animals do not breathe with lungs as humans do. Some invertebrates, such as earthworms and sea slugs, take oxygen in directly through their skin. Others use featherlike structures called **gills**. Gills work best in water because they have to be moist to keep their shape. That is one reason pill bugs live in moist places on land, such as under rocks.

The fingerlike projections on the back of this sea slug are gills. Each projection is made of specialized cells that work together to take in oxygen from the water.

Invertebrate Groups

There is more than one way to **classify** invertebrates. Scientists often disagree about the best way to do this. There are about 35 different **phyla** of animals and most of them include invertebrates.

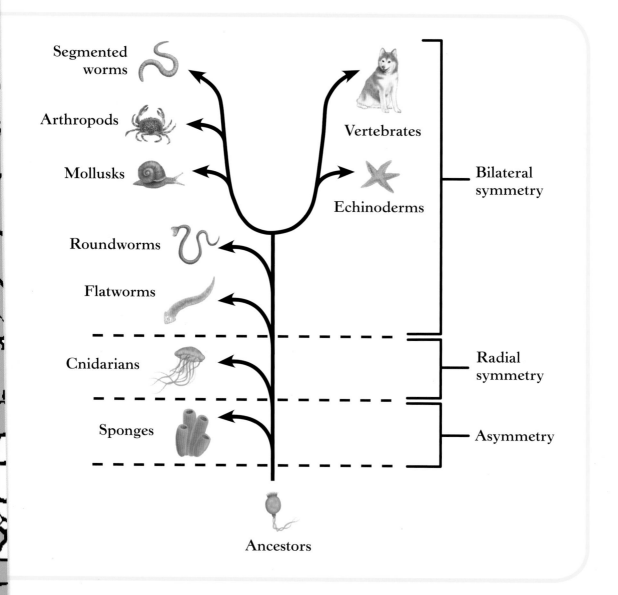

The diagram above shows one way that scientists think the different phyla of animals might be related to one another. Notice that the diagram has a tree shape. Each branch of the tree shows a group of animals. Branches that are close to one another, such as **segmented** worms and **arthropods**, show groups that are closely related. Branches that are far apart show animals, such as sponges and arthropods, that are not as closely related.

Discovering new invertebrates

Invertebrates make up at least 90 percent of all the species on Earth. More than one million different kinds of invertebrates are known, named, and classified. However, there are many, many more invertebrates yet to be found and classified. Some scientists think that there are more than five million still to be discovered.

To find new invertebrates, scientists search for animals in different places all over the world. They often take examples of these animals back to the laboratory to study and to compare with other known animals. Part of their work is to determine how these animals are all related to one another and how to best classify them into groups.

This table shows the main phyla of invertebrates and gives some examples of **species** in each phylum. Each of these phyla is discussed later in this book.

Phylum	Examples	Number of species
Sponges	glass sponges, calcareous sponges, demosponges	5,000
Cnidarians	hydras, Portuguese men-of war, corals, sea anemones, jellyfish	10,000
Flatworms	tapeworms, planarians, blood flukes, liver flukes	20,000
Roundworms (Nematodes)	hookworms, pinworms, whipworms, lungworms, threadworms, eelworms	15,000
Segmented worms (Annelids)	earthworms, polychaetes, leeches	20,000
Mollusks	clams, scallops, snails, slugs, octopuses, squid, nautiluses	100,000
Arthropods	insects, crabs, lobsters, pill bugs, spiders, scorpions, ticks, mites	1,200,000
Echinoderms	starfish, sea lilies, brittle stars, sea urchins, sand dollars, sea cucumbers	6,500

Sponges look a lot like plants. At one time, they were even **classified** as plants. They do not have arms, legs, eyes, ears, a head, or even a brain. However, sponges are animals. Their **cells** and habits are like those of other animals. Most sponges live in salty seawater, but a few live in freshwater ponds and lakes. There are about 5,000 **species** of sponges.

Unlike most other animals, the majority of sponges do not have **symmetry**. Their body parts do not grow around a central point or line. Their bodies cannot be divided into mirror images. Sponges are **asymmetric**.

Classifying sponges

Sponges are grouped into **classes** based on the chemicals that make up their skeleton. Sponges vary widely in shape, color, and size. The skeleton keeps the sponge's shape and allows water to flow into and out of the sponge.

Most sponge skeletons are squishy. Their skeletons are made of a chemical called spongin. Other sponges have a hard or brittle skeleton. Their skeletons are made of tiny needles, called spicules.

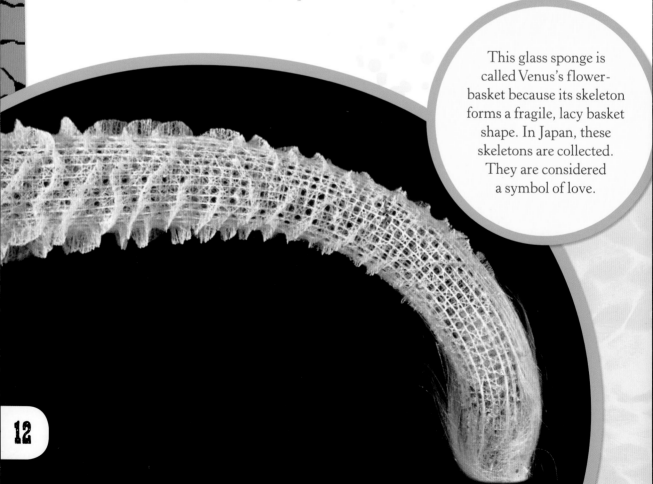

This glass sponge is called Venus's flower-basket because its skeleton forms a fragile, lacy basket shape. In Japan, these skeletons are collected. They are considered a symbol of love.

Staying in one place

Young sponge **larva** can swim. They swim away from the parent sponge and attach to a surface. Then they grow into an adult sponge. Adult sponges remain attached to the sand on the sea bottom, to rocks, to shells, or to other things under the water. They do not move around from place to place. Animals that do not move are **sessile**.

Water flowing in and out

Sponges do not have **tissues** or **organs**, but their cells do work together mainly to move water through the animal's body in one direction.

Water enters the sponge through small holes in the sponge's skin. Specialized cells with tiny hairs line the inside of the sponge's body. The movement of the hairs pulls water into the cells. The cells then trap tiny **organisms** in the water, such as **bacteria** and **algae**, and use them for food. The water then exits the sponge through a larger hole in the top. The water flow helps the sponge get food and oxygen, get rid of waste, and mate.

Did you know ... sponges can regenerate themselves?

If part of a sponge is cut off or damaged, it will grow back. This is called regeneration. In fact, a new adult sponge can grow back from only a few cells of the original sponge. The cells attach to a surface, such as a rock. Then they multiply and grow into a new, whole sponge.

This sponge is actively filtering food from seawater. It does this by pulling water into its body through tiny holes in its skin. The water later leaves the sponge through the larger holes that you can see here.

Cnidarians

Cnidarians include corals, hydras, jellyfish, Portuguese man-of-wars, sea anemones, and sea fans. Cnidarians live mostly in tropical waters. There are about 10,000 **species** of cnidarians.

The body of a cnidarian is arranged around a central point like the spokes on a bicycle wheel. You can divide a cnidarian into mirror images by drawing a line through the central point. They have **radial symmetry**. Animals like cnidarians that have radial symmetry do not have a front side or a back side. They also do not have a left side or a right side. They have only a top and a bottom.

All cnidarians have long **tentacles**. At the end of each tentacle is a stinging **cell**. Cnidarians are **carnivores** (meat-eaters). They use their tentacles to catch other small animals for food in the water around them. Larger cnidarians, such as jellyfish and sea anemones, eat small fish and hermit crabs.

Corals and sea anemones

Cnidarians have two body forms: **polyps** and **medusas**. Polyps are shaped like a vase. Corals and sea anemones have a polyp body form. A polyp is **sessile**. It stays attached to something under the water.

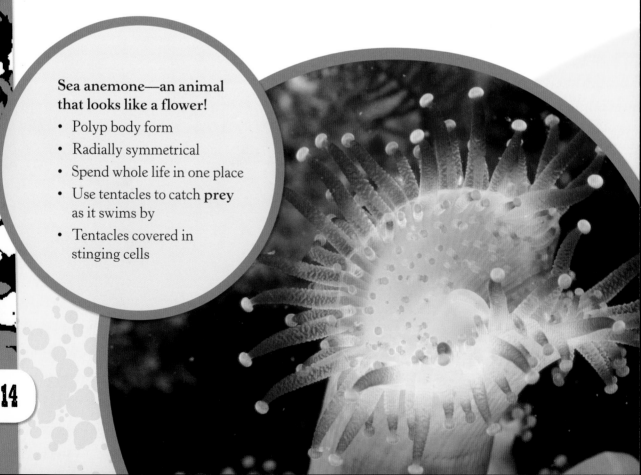

Sea anemone—an animal that looks like a flower!

- Polyp body form
- Radially symmetrical
- Spend whole life in one place
- Use tentacles to catch **prey** as it swims by
- Tentacles covered in stinging cells

Most polyps are soft, like sea anemones, but coral polyps make a hard limestone skeleton, which remains even when the polyps die. Over time, millions of coral skeletons build up to form a coral reef. These reefs are home to thousands of different species of sea creatures.

Jellyfish

Jellyfish have both polyp and medusa body forms during their life cycle. A medusa is shaped like an umbrella with tentacles that dangle below it. The jellyfish we see floating in the ocean and washed up on beaches are medusas. Before these jellyfish were medusas, they were tiny polyps attached to the ocean floor. Jellyfish polyps make medusas that break away from the polyp. The polyp stays behind, where it makes more medusas.

Poisonous jellies

The poison produced by the stinging cells on the tentacles of most cnidarians has little or no effect on people. However, some of these invertebrates can cause terrible rashes and even death. The Portuguese man-of-war is an example.

Flatworms

Flatworms make up a **phylum** of simple worms with soft, flattened bodies. The body of a flatworm can be divided into two halves. This kind of **symmetry** is called **bilateral symmetry**. Flatworms have a head as well as a top and a bottom side.

Free-living flatworms

Most free-living flatworms, also known as turbellarians, are tiny. Nearly all of them are less than 5 millimeters (0.2 inch) long. Some are microscopic. The largest members of this group are the planarians. Some planarians can grow about as long as your arm, about 0.5 meter long (about 20 inches).

Flukes

Flukes tend to live in humans and other animals. They are **parasites**. Usually, these parasites get food from the **host** animal. Many flukes live in the blood vessels or livers of their hosts, making the host sick. Some kinds of flukes that infect people pass one stage of their life cycle in snails. Often, people get these worms by swimming or working in water where infected snails live. To get rid of the worms, a person can take medicine.

Planarians—flatworms of the soil and water
- Prefer darkness
- When they swim, the body moves in a wavelike motion
- Have two simple eyes, which sense light and dark
- Are often **carnivores**, eating protozoa, small snails, and other worms

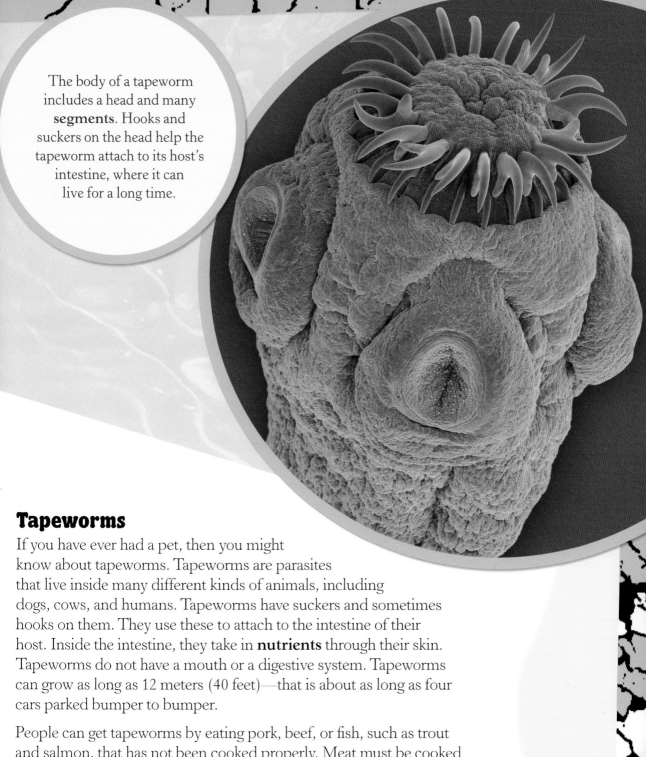

The body of a tapeworm includes a head and many **segments**. Hooks and suckers on the head help the tapeworm attach to its host's intestine, where it can live for a long time.

Tapeworms

If you have ever had a pet, then you might know about tapeworms. Tapeworms are parasites that live inside many different kinds of animals, including dogs, cows, and humans. Tapeworms have suckers and sometimes hooks on them. They use these to attach to the intestine of their host. Inside the intestine, they take in **nutrients** through their skin. Tapeworms do not have a mouth or a digestive system. Tapeworms can grow as long as 12 meters (40 feet)—that is about as long as four cars parked bumper to bumper.

People can get tapeworms by eating pork, beef, or fish, such as trout and salmon, that has not been cooked properly. Meat must be cooked so that it is hot all the way through. This will kill the tapeworm **larvae** that might be living there. If live tapeworm larvae are in the meat, they can attach to the intestine of a person who eats the meat and live there for a long time. To get rid of tapeworms, a person has to either take medicine to kill the tapeworms or have them removed with surgery.

There are about 15,000 known **species** of roundworms. Some scientists estimate that there may be as many as 750,000 species of roundworms. Roundworms include many common **parasites**, such as hookworms, pinworms, whipworms, and lungworms. They infect humans, pigs, dogs, cats, and other animals in different ways. Most roundworm infections can be cured with medicine.

Most roundworms are too small to be seen with your eyes alone. The largest roundworm can grow to about 8 meters (25 feet) long—as long as a small school bus. Roundworms have **bilateral symmetry**. The body of a roundworm looks like a pencil that has been sharpened on both ends.

Hookworms

In some parts of the world—even in the United States—going barefoot can allow tiny threadlike hookworm **larvae** to pass into your body through the skin of your feet. You do not have to have an open sore; the worms go through the skin. Once inside the body, they make their way to the intestine where they live by sucking blood. Hookworms infect dogs, cats, and humans.

Hookworms—a parasite
- On average about 10 mm (0.4 in) long
- Live in human intestines
- Make thousands of eggs
- Eggs leave body in feces
- Hatch out in soil
- Get into body of new host by burrowing through skin of feet

Worms in meat

The larvae of small roundworms are sometimes found in pork and other meat. These larvae have a hard outer coating. When a person eats meat that has not been cooked enough, he or she also eats the roundworm larvae. Once inside the person's intestines, the outer coating of the worm larvae is **digested** and the worms begin to grow. By getting in the bloodstream, they can live throughout a person's body and cause a disease called trichinosis.

As many as one in five of all Americans are infected with these roundworms. Most people do not have enough roundworms to make them sick. The best way to avoid getting trichinosis is to make sure that meat is completely cooked before eating it. This kills the larvae. People who have trichinosis usually have stomach cramps for several months, but the infection rarely requires treatment.

Intestinal worms

Ascaris worms are large. They can grow as long as 30 centimeters (12 inches) long in the human intestine. Some scientists think that these worms are the most common human parasite. They enter the body when a person eats any food that has the worm's eggs on it. Often these eggs are found on vegetables in areas with poor sanitation. They can also get in the body from a person's hands. That's one reason washing food and your hands before eating is so important.

Animals are common hosts to roundworm parasites. These roundworms have infected an African rock python. You can protect your pets from roundworms by giving them medicine from a veterinarian.

19

Segmented Worms

There are about 20,000 known **species** of **segmented** worms. Some are less than 1 millimeter (0.04 inch) long—that is about as long as a dime is thick. Other segmented worms grow to 3 meters (10 feet) long! That's longer than the distance from the floor to the ceiling in most schools. They live underground, in lakes and ponds, and in all the oceans of the world. All segmented worms have **bilateral symmetry**. Their bodies are divided into almost identical rings, similar to those that make up an earthworm.

Earthworms

Earthworms live in the tunnels they eat through soil. Earthworms are good for the soil because they break the soil into small pieces and add air to it. This makes it easier for plants to grow. They use stiff bristles called **setae** to hold on to the soil. Over a million earthworms might live in one acre of rich soil.

As it digs, the soil moves into the earthworm's mouth. It then moves down the long digestive tube to the **gizzard**. The gizzard grinds up the soil, and **nutrients** from the soil pass into the bloodstream. These nutrients are distributed to all of the body **cells**.

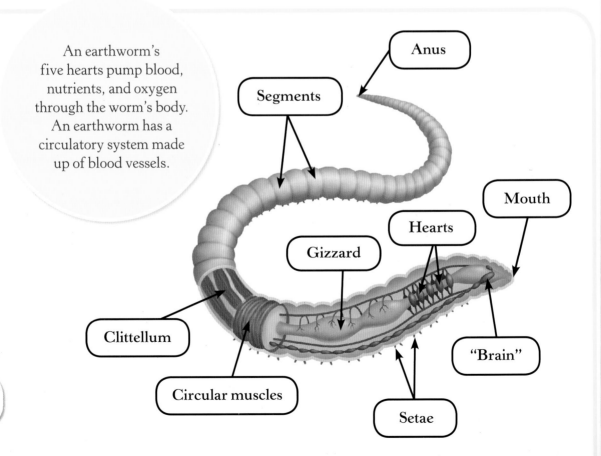

An earthworm's five hearts pump blood, nutrients, and oxygen through the worm's body. An earthworm has a circulatory system made up of blood vessels.

Anus

Segments

Mouth

Hearts

Gizzard

Clittellum

"Brain"

Circular muscles

Setae

Blood suckers

Leeches are segmented worms that have flat bodies and suckers on both ends of their bodies. Some leeches use their suckers to suck blood from other animals. They are mostly small worms, about 2.5–5 centimeters (1–2 inches) long. But the giant Amazon leech can grow to about 0.5 meter (20 inches)—about the length of a computer keyboard.

Leeches bite their **host** to draw blood. Leech **saliva** contains chemicals that numb the place where they bite. These chemicals keep the bite area from hurting, increase the blood flow, and prevent blood clotting. Doctors sometimes use these chemicals to treat wounds on patients.

Did you know ... doctors really do use leeches?

Centuries ago leeches were a regular medical treatment. "Bleeding" a patient using leeches was one of the few things a physician could do. You might be surprised to find that even in the 21st century, surgeons still sometimes use leeches. One example is when surgeons reconnect a body part, such as a finger that has been accidentally cut off. When this happens, the heart pumps blood to the newly attached finger, but blood vessels in the finger do not work well at first. Until the finger's blood vessels heal, a leech can suck the extra blood out of the finger. Without the leech's blood sucking, blood could pool in the finger, causing the finger to die.

Mollusks include snails, oysters, squid, and octopuses. They make up the second largest animal **phylum**. There are more than 100,000 mollusk **species**. They live on land and in the water. Most live in shells, but some do not. Most have **bilateral symmetry**.

Mollusk bodies are made up of three main parts: a foot, a **visceral mass**, and a mantle. The foot is a muscle used for movement. The visceral mass contains the animal's **organs**. The mantle covers the visceral mass like skin. In some mollusks, the mantle makes a protective shell around the animal's main body. All mollusks, except those with two shells, have a head and tonguelike organ, called a radula.

Two-shelled mollusks

About 10,000 species of mollusks have two shells attached to each other. These mollusks are called **bivalves** and include oysters, mussels, and clams.

Muscles connect the two shells and can open and close them. These animals do not have a head, but they do have a simple brain.

Two-shelled mollusks get food by sucking in water through a hollow tube called a siphon. The water moves in through one tube, flows over the **gills**, and leaves the animal through another tube. As water flows over the mollusk's gills, tiny animals in the water are trapped in a sticky **mucus** covering the gills. Tiny hairs on the gills move the food to the mollusk's mouth. This type of feeding is called filter feeding.

Snails—a garden pest
- Gastropod mollusk
- Coiled shell produced by mantle
- Mantle invisible inside shell
- Head and foot stick out of shell when snail is moving
- The organs (visceral mass) found inside the shell

One-shelled mollusks

One-shelled mollusks are called **gastropods**. They include about 80,000 species of snails and slugs. Most have one shell, although modern slugs either have a small internal shell or no shell at all.

Most gastropods live in seawater, but some live in freshwater and on land. Land snails produce a slimy substance. This helps them glide across surfaces. Gastropods use their radula to scrape **algae** off rocks, to cut leaves off garden plants, and even to drill holes in the shells of other mollusks.

Big-headed mollusks

Cephalopods (which means "head-foot") include about 600 species of squid, octopuses, cuttlefishes, and nautiluses. Most cephalopods do not have an external shell, although many have a small internal shell-like structure. The nautilus is the only living cephalopod that has a shell. They have very good eyes. In fact, the giant squid has the largest eyes ever measured. One eye can be 40 centimeters (16 inches) across, larger than a dinner plate.

The foot part of their body is divided into arms or **tentacles**. Squid have eight arms and two tentacles. Octopuses have eight arms. Nautiluses can have 80 or 90 tentacles! They all eat fish, worms, and other sea animals.

Cephalopod mollusks, like this octopus, are the most intelligent invertebrate animals.

Arthropods

Arthropods include insects, spiders, crabs, and lobsters. If you were to fill a bag with leaves from the forest floor, you would find hundreds of arthropods, including insects, mites, ticks, spiders, and pill bugs.

Some biologists believe that arthropods **evolved** from **segmented** worms. Like segmented worms, arthropods also have segmented bodies. In many arthropods, the body segments are fused together into a head, a **thorax**, and an **abdomen**. Arthropods have legs and other **appendages** that are jointed, which allows them to move around. They have **bilateral symmetry**. Their bodies are encased in an **exoskeleton**.

Six-legged arthropods

Insects include beetles, ants, bees, wasps, roaches, termites, butterflies, moths, mosquitoes, crickets, dragonflies, fleas, and lice. Most living things on Earth are insects.

Insects have three pairs of legs that are connected to the thorax. Like other arthropods, insect legs have joints that allow them to bend. Some also have one or two pairs of wings. Insects are the only arthropods that can fly.

As they **molt** and grow, the bodies of insects change in a process called metamorphosis. Young grasshoppers look similar to adult grasshoppers, but they cannot fly or reproduce. Young butterflies are caterpillars and look very different from adult butterflies.

The changes an insect goes through during its life are called **metamorphoses**. Some insects undergo incomplete metamorphosis when the young insects look similar to the adults. Others undergo complete metamorphosis. This is when the **larvae** look completely different from the adult, for example, caterpillars that become butterflies.

Insects are very important in many ways. They **pollinate** flowers and so enable fruit to grow. They eat food grown for people—up to a third of all crops are destroyed by pests and many of them are insects.

Insects are found in almost every environment on Earth, although relatively few are found in the oceans.

Eight-legged land dwellers

Arachnids include spiders, mites, ticks, chiggers, and scorpions. They have eight walking legs, and mouthparts in the form of either fangs or pincers. The head and thorax are joined into one segment called a **cephalothorax**. The main body **organs** are in the abdomen.

Most spiders, like this *Argiope*, spin webs. The web is made of sticky thread produced by the spider. **Prey** gets caught in the web, and the spider will eat the prey later.

Most **arachnids** live on land. Almost all arachnids are **carnivores**. Because they have no jaws, arachnids can eat only liquid food. After they crush their **prey**, these animals usually shoot a chemical into the prey's body, or apply digestive juices to it. This chemical turns the prey's body into liquid, which the arachnid can then suck up.

Insects of the sea

Crustaceans are as plentiful in water as insects are on land. They include lobsters, crayfish, shrimps, crabs, barnacles, water fleas, and pill bugs. For this reason, they have been called the "insects of the sea." All crustaceans, even those living on land, breathe through **gills** Crustacean legs, claws, and **antennae** are branched. They have two pairs of antennae and three mouthparts used for chewing. They have legs attached to their **abdomen** and **thorax**.

Crayfish have ten legs. The front pair of legs are pincers. Tiny projections off the abdomen, called swimmerets, are used in swimming and **reproduction**. These animals swim by bending their abdomen.

Echinoderms include starfish, sea lilies, brittle stars, sand dollars, sea urchins, and sea cucumbers. All of these animals live in the ocean. They begin as **larvae** with **bilateral symmetry**. However, as adults, echinoderms have **radial symmetry** and no head.

All echinoderms have an **endoskeleton**, which is made hard by **calcium**. Instead of bones, the echinoderm endoskeleton is made up of hard plates, which are covered by skin.

Star-shaped animals

Starfish are meat-eating **predators**. They eat clams, mussels, corals, and sometimes even other starfish. Starfish use their tube feet to pry open mollusk shells, and then push one of their two stomachs into the shell to **digest** the animal inside.

Starfish can grow back an arm that breaks off. Any part that is attached to the central part of the starfish can grow back. One starfish arm that is still attached to even a piece of the central part can grow back a whole starfish—which results in two starfish. Even if a starfish loses all of its arms, the central part can grow them all back. It is a very slow process, and can take as long as one year.

Starfish are not the only star-shaped animals. Brittle stars and feather stars also have this shape. Sand dollars lack arms, but you can see the star shape on their surface.

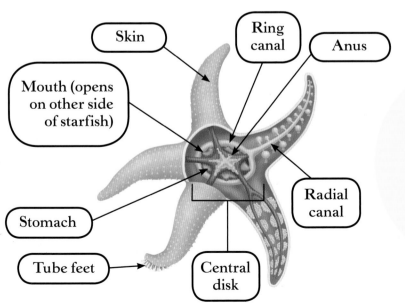

Skin

Ring canal

Anus

Mouth (opens on other side of starfish)

Radial canal

Stomach

Tube feet

Central disk

Most starfish have five-part radial symmetry. This means that the body extends in five different directions from a central point.

The number of different types of living **organisms** in the world is often called the **biodiversity**. Sadly, all over the world, **species** of living organisms are becoming **extinct**. This means that these organisms no longer exist on Earth. There are many different reasons for this. Extinction has always happened— some species die out and other species **evolve**. But today people are changing the world in ways that affect all other species.

Coral reefs—a dying breed?

Coral **polyps** may be tiny but they create massive coral reefs—the Great Barrier Reef can be seen from space. A huge variety of animal life is linked to the reefs, with invertebrates ranging from sea anemones to octopuses and **vertebrates** including fish of many different colors, shapes, and sizes. However, human activities, such as sewage pollution, are killing many coral reefs. Global warming is another threat, with reefs dying off at a rapid rate. Almost half of all the species of corals that build reefs are threatened with extinction. And if coral reefs go, thousands of species that depend on them and millions of people will be affected.

This reef in Costa Rica has been bleached.

This is a healthy coral reef in the Red Sea.

These ammonites are the fossils of early mollusks, which were quite similar to the modern Nautilus.

People are destroying the places where animals live. We are cutting down rain forests and polluting the air and the water. Our use of fossil fuels, such as oil and gas, is causing global warming. Global warming is a rise in Earth's average temperature and a change in weather patterns. When the temperature and the weather change, it can have a serious effect on living things.

Many types of invertebrates have remained relatively unchanged for thousands of years. Yet with the changes that are taking place, many may not survive for you to show your grandchildren!

Early invertebrate **fossils** show that these animals have been around for at least 500 million years. The invertebrates include an amazing range of species, many of which appear to have survived almost unchanged since prehistoric times. It would be a tragedy if these ancient species were to disappear now. Modern invertebrates are a vital part of the world's ecosystems—especially for **pollinating** crops that we need for food.

What can be done?

To help prevent invertebrates from becoming extinct, people need to look after Earth better. If global warming can be stopped, many species will be saved. It is important to protect the places where invertebrates live—which is almost everywhere. Biodiversity is important—we need as many species of invertebrates as possible for the future.

Glossary

abdomen part of an arthropod's body that lies behind the thorax

algae plants that do not have roots, stems, or leaves and live in water or damp soil

ancestor relative that lived millions of years ago

antenna (plural is **antennae**) long, thin organ used to sense the environment

anus opening in the body through which waste leaves

appendage legs, claws, antennae, and other body parts that extend off the main part of the body

arachnid eight-legged arthropod

arthropod segmented animal that has an exoskeleton and jointed legs

asymmetric having no regular body pattern

bacteria single-celled organism that does not have a nucleus

bilateral symmetry each half of an organism's body is identical

biodiversity different types of organisms around the world

bivalve mollusk that has two shells

calcium chemical that is necessary for most plants and animals to survive

carnivore organism that eats meat

cell smallest unit of life

cephalopod mollusk that has eight or more arms around the mouth and usually does not have a shell

cephalothorax body region in arthropods that includes the head and the thorax fused together

class level of classification that contains similar orders

classify group organisms into categories based on their similar characteristics

crustacean arthropod that has an exoskeleton and usually lives in water

digest break down food so it can be used by the body

echinoderm invertebrate that does not have a head and lives in the water

endoskeleton hard skeleton inside an animal's body

evolve change over time

exoskeleton hard skeleton on the outside of an animal's body

extinct die out

family level of classification that contains similar genera

fossil remains of organisms that once lived on Earth

gastropod mollusk that usually has one shell

gene structure by which all living things pass on characteristics to the next generation

genus (plural is **genera**) level of classification grouping between family and species

gill organ used by water-living animals to get oxygen

gizzard muscular part of the digestive tube in which food is churned and ground up

host animal on which a parasite lives and feeds from

hydrostatic skeleton sac filled with liquid inside an animal's body

kingdom level of classification that contains similar phylum

larva (plural is **larvae**) wingless form of newly hatched insects

medusa umbrella-shaped, free-swimming body form of a cnidarian

metamorphosis change. Insects change as they grow into adults.

molt shed an exoskeleton

mucus slime

multicellular having many cells

nutrient chemical that helps animals carry out life processes

order level of classification grouping between class and family

organ group of tissues that work together to carry out a certain job

organism living thing

parasite living thing that lives and feeds on or inside another living thing

phylum (plural is **phyla**) level of classification that contains similar classes

pollinating transferring of pollen from male to female flower parts

polyp stalklike body form of a cnidarian

predator animal that hunts and eats other animals

prey animal that is hunted and eaten by other animals

pupa (plural is **pupae**) stage in complete metamorphosis between a larva and an adult

radial symmetry body form in which, no matter how the body is divided, there will always be two identical parts

reproduce produce another living thing of the same kind

saliva liquid in the mouth that breaks down food

segment small piece of a larger whole

sessile unable to move about

seta (plural is **setae**) organ used by earthworms to move

species level of classification that contains similar organisms

symmetry body form or pattern of a plant or animal

tentacle long, armlike structure that is used to capture prey

thorax middle section of an arthropod's body

tissue group of cells working together to carry out a certain job

vertebrate animal that has a backbone

visceral mass digestive, waste-removing, and circulatory structures

Find Out More

Burnie, David. *e.Encyclopedia Animal*. New York: DK Children, 2005.

Parker, Steve. *Sponges, Jellyfish, and Other Simple Animals*. Mankato, Minn.: Compass Point, 2006.

Solway, Andrew. *Spiders and Other Invertebrates*. Chicago: Heinemann Library, 2006.

Index